All About Leopard Geckos

Your Comprehensive Guide to Leopard Gecko Ownership

The leopard gecko (Eublepharis macularius) is one of the most popular lizard species in the world of reptile breeding, and rightly so. With its vibrant colors, unique patterns, and docile temperament, the leopard gecko has captured the imagination of reptile enthusiasts for decades. But behind its external beauty there is also a series of needs and characteristics that require a thorough understanding to ensure its well-being in captivity.

In this guide, we take a clear and concise approach to answering all your leopard gecko questions. Whether you want to know how to create the ideal terrarium, what is the best diet for your gecko, or how to interpret its behaviors, you will find all the answers here, presented in an accessible and easy to understand way.

Whether you're new to the world of reptiles or a seasoned breeder looking for additional guidance, "The Leopard Gecko: Complete Question-Answer Guide" is your ultimate handbook for all things related to these magnificent lizards. Get ready to dive into a world of fascinating discoveries and become a leopard gecko expert!

SUMMARY

What is a leopard gecko? 7

leopard geckos ? 7

What is the average size of an adult leopard gecko? 8

How long does a leopard gecko live in captivity? 8

What is the difference between a leopard gecko and a lizard? 8

Does a leopard gecko require a vertical or horizontal terrarium? 9

Do leopard geckos need UVB light? 9

What temperature should it be in a leopard gecko's terrarium? 10

What is a leopard gecko's diet? 10

What substrate is most suitable for a leopard gecko terrarium? 11

How often should you feed a leopard gecko? 12

What are the signs of illness in leopard geckos? 12

When is the breeding season for leopard geckos? 13

How long does gestation last in leopard geckos? 13

Can leopard geckos be kept together? 13

How to tell a male from a female leopard gecko? 14

Can leopard geckos molt? 15

How often do leopard geckos shed? 15

How long can a leopard gecko go without eating? 16

How do leopard geckos communicate with each other? 16

Do leopard geckos like to be handled? 17

geckos hibernate? 17

What are the natural predators of leopard geckos? 18

Are leopard geckos suitable pets for children? 18

Are leopard geckos noisy animals? 19

geckos have teeth? 19

Can leopard geckos climb glass surfaces? 19

Can leopard geckos be trained? 19

Can leopard geckos lose their tails? 20

What is the average price of a leopard gecko?...20

Can leopard geckos be kept in a terrarium with live plants? 21

What are the differences between leopard geckos and leopard geckos? 21

Are leopard geckos prone to parasites? 22

Are leopard geckos aggressive? 22

Do leopard geckos like water? 23

Can leopard geckos change color ?...23

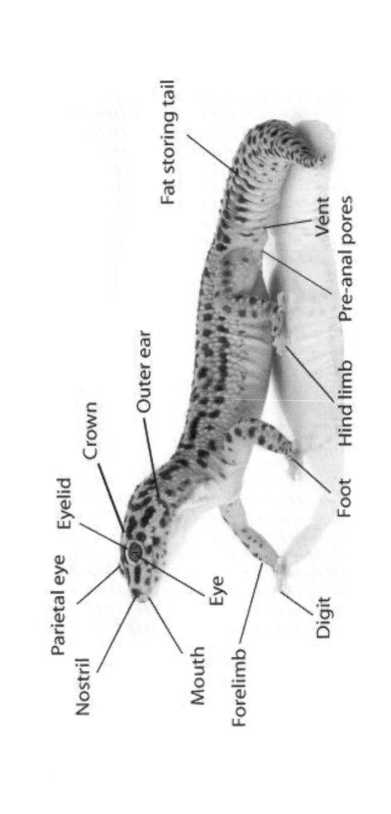

What is a leopard gecko?

The leopard gecko (Eublepharis macularius) is a species of lizard native to arid and semi-arid regions of Afghanistan, Iran, Pakistan and India. It is widely bred in captivity due to its vibrant coloration, unique patterns, and docile temperament. Unlike many other gecko species, the leopard gecko is terrestrial rather than arboreal, meaning it prefers to move on the ground rather than climb branches. It is also known to be one of the few gecko species that has movable eyelids, allowing them to blink. These lizards are popular among reptile enthusiasts due to their ease of care and adaptability to captivity.

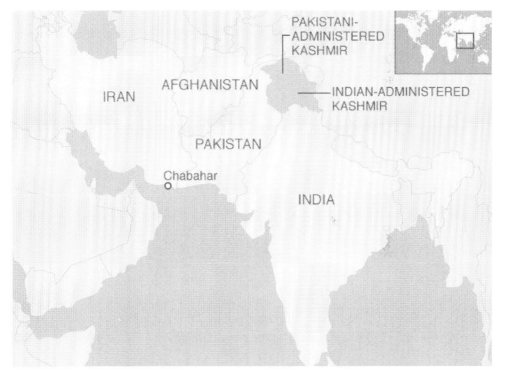

What is the origin of leopard gecko ?

The leopard gecko (Eublepharis macularius) is native to arid and semi-arid regions of Asia, including Afghanistan, Iran, Pakistan and India. These terrestrial lizards are typically found in rocky, desert, or semi-desert habitats. Unlike many other geckos, leopard geckos do not have adhesive lamellae under their toes, which prevents them from climbing smooth surfaces like other gecko species do. This characteristic, along with their relatively docile temperament and ease of care, makes them popular as pets around the world.

What is the average size of an adult leopard gecko?

The average size of an adult leopard gecko generally ranges between 15 and 25 centimeters in total length, from the tip of the snout to the tip of the tail. However, it should be noted that sizes may vary slightly depending on various factors, such as the age, gender and genetics of the individual. Some specimens may be slightly larger or smaller than this average, but most adult leopard geckos fall within this size range.

How long does a leopard gecko live in captivity?

In captivity, the average lifespan of a well-cared for and properly housed leopard gecko is generally 10 to 20 years, or even longer in some cases. With proper living conditions, a balanced diet, and regular veterinary care, these lizards can live relatively long and healthy lives in captivity.

What is the difference between a leopard gecko and a lizard?

The leopard gecko is a specific species of lizard (Eublepharis macularius), which is distinguished by its average size of approximately 15 to 25 centimeters, its granular skin, its mobile eyelids and its absence of adhesive lamellae under the fingers. Unlike many other geckos, it is terrestrial and prefers arid or semi-arid habitats. Native to Asia, including Afghanistan, Iran, Pakistan and India, the leopard gecko is differentiated from other lizards by its distinctive physical characteristics and habitat preferences.

Does a leopard gecko require a vertical or horizontal terrarium?

A horizontal terrarium is generally more suitable for a leopard gecko. Leopard geckos are terrestrial lizards that prefer to explore their environment at ground level. A horizontal terrarium therefore offers them more space to move around and express themselves naturally. Make sure the terrarium is large enough for your leopard gecko to move around comfortably and also provides hiding places and structures for climbing, as although they are primarily terrestrial, they may enjoy climbing from time to time. In summary, a horizontal terrarium with generous floor space and climbing opportunities is optimal for the well-being of a leopard gecko.

Do leopard geckos need UVB light?

Leopard geckos do not require UVB light in the same way as some other reptile species. Unlike many lizards that are active during the day and require UVB light for vitamin D3 synthesis, leopard geckos are primarily active during the night or dusk, and they generally absorb most of their nutrients, including including vitamin D3, from their diet.

However, a small amount of UVB light can still be beneficial for leopard geckos, as it can help stimulate their appetite, strengthen their immune system, and support their overall well-being. If you choose to use a UVB lamp, make sure it is low wattage (e.g. 2-5%) and is on for a few hours a day.

What temperature should it be in a leopard gecko's terrarium?

Terrarium temperature is a crucial aspect of leopard gecko well-being. During the day, it is recommended to maintain an ambient temperature in the range of 26 to 30 degrees Celsius (approximately 79 to 86 degrees Fahrenheit) in the warm zone of the terrarium. The nighttime temperature may drop slightly, but it should not drop below 20 degrees Celsius (about 68 degrees Fahrenheit) to ensure the gecko's thermal comfort. To create a proper thermal gradient, a warm zone with a temperature of 30 to 32 degrees Celsius (about 86 to 90 degrees Fahrenheit) should be maintained, allowing the gecko to warm up as needed. It is imperative to regularly monitor the temperature of the terrarium using thermometers placed in different locations to ensure an optimal environment for the health and well-being of your leopard gecko.

What is a leopard gecko's diet?

A captive leopard gecko's diet consists primarily of insects and other small invertebrates. Common foods given to leopard geckos include crickets, mealworms, silkworms, cockroaches, grasshoppers, and earthworms. It is also important to vary their diet to ensure adequate nutritional intake. Some owners also feed their leopard geckos vitamin and mineral dietary supplements to ensure they get all the nutrients they need.

How to handle a leopard gecko safely?

To handle a leopard gecko safely, a gentle and respectful approach is essential. First, make sure the gecko is aware of your presence by slowly approaching it. When handling him, use slow, gentle movements to avoid stressing him. It is important to properly support your body and paws during handling, avoiding grabbing or squeezing too hard. Keep in mind not to handle its tail, as it can come off easily if stressed. Pay attention to the gecko's stress signals, such as startles or attempts to escape, and stop handling if necessary. By following these tips and handling your gecko carefully, you can build trust and ensure their well-being while handling them safely.

Should leopard geckos be fed live prey?

Yes, in general leopard geckos should be fed live prey to ensure they receive adequate nutrition and stimulate their natural hunting behavior. Live prey such as crickets, mealworms, silkworms, cockroaches, and grasshoppers make up a large part of the diet of leopard geckos in captivity. Live prey provides essential nutrients and stimulates the gecko's physical and mental activity.

However, some leopard geckos may accept dead prey, particularly if they are accustomed to eating it from a young age. In this case, it is important to ensure that the dead prey is fresh and uncontaminated to avoid any health problems for the gecko.

What substrate is most suitable for a leopard gecko terrarium?

The most suitable substrate for a leopard gecko terrarium is generally a non-toxic, hygienic and safe substrate, which can help maintain humidity while avoiding the risk of accidental ingestion. Leopard gecko owners often opt for substrates such as coir, paper towels, newspaper, or coir felt mats. Coir is popular because it retains moisture well, which is beneficial for crested geckos, which need adequate humidity levels in their habitat. Additionally, coconut fiber is relatively safe if accidentally ingested by the gecko.

Regardless of the substrate chosen, it is important to ensure that it is free of harmful chemicals and does not pose risks of ingestion or negative impact on the leopard gecko's health.

How often should you feed a leopard gecko?

The feeding frequency of leopard geckos varies depending on their age, size and health. Young, growing geckos need more food than adults and can be fed every day or every other day to ensure optimal growth. Once adults, leopard geckos may be fed less frequently, usually two to three times per week, to maintain a healthy body weight. It is important to monitor your gecko's weight to adjust feeding frequency accordingly. Additionally, offering a variety of insects and live prey helps ensure a balanced nutritional intake. Remember to sprinkle prey with appropriate vitamin and mineral supplements to meet your leopard gecko's nutritional needs.

What are the signs of illness in leopard geckos?

Identifying signs of illness in leopard geckos is essential to ensuring their health and well-being. Several signs can indicate health problems in these lizards. First of all, monitoring your leopard gecko's appetite is crucial; a loss of appetite or a significant decrease in food intake may be the first indicator of illness. Likewise, unexplained weight loss is a serious concern and requires immediate attention.

Behavioral changes, such as lethargy, unusual aggression, or social withdrawal, can also indicate health problems. On a physical level, symptoms such as skin lesions, swelling, stool abnormalities or body deformities should be taken seriously. Difficulty breathing, eye problems, such as swollen or irritated eyes, and dehydration are also potential signs of illness in leopard geckos. Finally, the presence of external parasites, such as dust mites, can also indicate an underlying health problem. If you observe any of these signs in your leopard gecko, it is recommended that you consult a reptile veterinarian as soon as possible for proper diagnosis and treatment. Acting quickly can help maximize the chances of recovery and maintain the long-term health of your leopard gecko.

When is the breeding season for leopard geckos?

In general, leopard geckos are capable of breeding throughout the year, but there is often a more active breeding season, which can vary depending on the region and local conditions.

In areas with distinct seasons, leopard geckos' breeding season may be most active in spring and summer, when temperatures rise and days are longer. However, in captivity, where environmental conditions are controlled, leopard geckos can breed at any time of the year. When breeding, males actively seek out females and perform courtship behaviors to attract their attention. If a female is receptive, she will allow a male to mate with her. Females may lay multiple clutches of eggs throughout the breeding season.

How long does gestation last in leopard geckos?

Leopard geckos do not carry their eggs in their bodies like some other reptiles do. Instead, females lay eggs after mating. The gestation period for leopard geckos refers to the time between mating and egg laying.

After mating, females can take between 15 and 22 days to lay their eggs. During this period, they often prepare a nest by digging into the terrarium substrate or using suitable hiding places. Once the eggs are laid, they are usually incubated for about 35 to 60 days, depending on the incubation temperature.

Can leopard geckos be kept together?

In general, it is not recommended to keep multiple leopard geckos together, especially adult males, due to the risk of aggressive and territorial behavior. Leopard geckos are solitary animals in the wild and may display territorial behaviors towards other members of their species, especially of the same sex. If you keep multiple leopard geckos in the same terrarium, you may see fights over territory, aggression, and even injuries.

However, it is possible to keep several females together, especially if they are raised together from a young age. In this case, be sure to provide a large enough space with plenty of hiding places and hotspots to avoid conflicts.

MALE   FEMALE

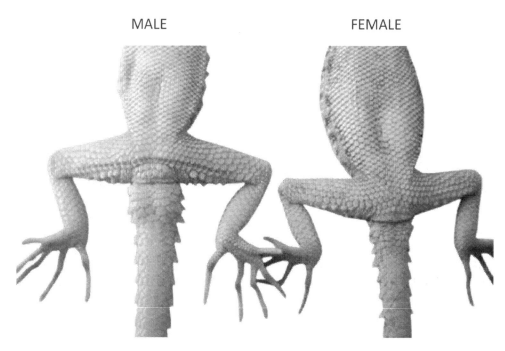

How to tell a male from a female leopard gecko?

There are several physical characteristics that help distinguish a male from a female leopard gecko. The most common differences are in:

Size : In general, males tend to be slightly larger than females, although this size difference can be subtle.

Base of tail : Males often have a broader and thicker base of tail than females, especially when mature.

The presence of femoral pores : Adult males generally have femoral pores, small V-shaped structures located on the inner side of the thighs, which secrete pheromones used in communication with females during reproduction. These pores are generally absent in females.

Head shape : Males may have slightly larger and more massive heads than females, although this difference can be subtle.

Behaviour : Adult males can sometimes exhibit territorial and aggressive behavior towards other males or even towards females during the breeding season.

Can leopard geckos molt?

Yes, leopard geckos shed regularly throughout their lives to allow for growth and renewal of their skin. Molting is a natural process in reptiles, including leopard geckos, that allows them to shed their old skin and replace it with a new coat. This process is important to maintain the health of their skin, ensure proper growth and allow for tissue regeneration.

How often do leopard geckos shed?

How often leopard geckos shed can vary depending on several factors, including their age, growth, health, and environmental conditions. In general, young leopard geckos shed more frequently than adults because they are growing and their skin renews more quickly. Adult geckos shed less frequently, but they will continue to shed throughout their lives to maintain healthy, functioning skin.

Typically, leopard geckos molt about once every 4 to 8 weeks. However, this frequency may vary from one individual to another. Some geckos may shed more frequently, while others may shed less often.

How long can a leopard gecko go without eating?

A leopard gecko can usually go without eating for a few weeks without suffering serious consequences, especially if it is healthy and well-fed beforehand. However, the length of time a leopard gecko can fast varies depending on several factors, including its age, health, size, and fat reserve.

Leopard geckos may fast for longer periods during winter months in response to cooler environmental conditions or decreased metabolic activity. Some leopard geckos may also fast during the shedding period. However, prolonged fasting can lead to excessive weight loss, weakness, dehydration and other health problems.

How do leopard geckos communicate with each other?

Leopard geckos communicate with each other primarily through visual, tactile, and chemical signals. The main ways they interact are:

Through visual communication : Leopard geckos often use visual signals to communicate, such as body postures, movements, and color changes. For example, during courtship , males may exhibit specific behaviors to attract the attention of females.

Through tactile communication : Leopard geckos can also communicate through touch. They may touch with their limbs or rub against each other to establish social contact or ease conflict.

Through chemical communication : Leopard geckos use pheromones to communicate chemically with their peers. Pheromones are chemicals released from scent glands located on the gecko's body, such as the femoral pores. These pheromones may play a role in recognizing sexual partners, demarcating territories, and other social interactions.

Vocalizations : Although leopard geckos do not produce sounds audible to the human ear, they can emit ultrasonic vocalizations or body vibrations to communicate with other geckos.

By combining these different modes of communication, leopard geckos can interact socially, establish territorial bonds, find breeding partners and maintain social dynamics in their environment.

Do leopard geckos like to be handled?

Leopard geckos are generally shy animals and prefer to avoid direct human interactions. Unlike some other pets, they do not actively seek contact with humans and may feel stressed or threatened when handled.

Although some leopard geckos can tolerate occasional handling, it is important to do so carefully and respect their limits. Too much handling can cause stress and disrupt their natural behavior.

geckos hibernate?

Leopard geckos do not hibernate in their natural habitat, as they are native to warm, tropical regions where temperatures remain relatively constant throughout the year. However, in captivity, some leopard geckos may enter a period of winter dormancy, similar to hibernation, in response to seasonal changes in temperature and light conditions.

This winter dormancy, sometimes called " brumation ," is typically observed in leopard geckos kept in conditions where temperatures and photoperiod (day length) are reduced during the winter months. During this period, the gecko's metabolic activity slows down, it may lose its appetite and spend most of its time resting in a cool, dark place in the terrarium.

What are the natural predators of leopard geckos?

In their natural habitat, leopard geckos face a variety of predators that may hunt them for food. These predators include **birds of prey** such as hawks and eagles, which are able to spot and capture leopard geckos from the air. **Snakes** , with their ability to squeeze through tight spaces, also pose a significant threat to leopard geckos, often chasing them into their own habitat. Additionally, **small mammals** like rats and mongooses, as well as some other reptiles, may also view leopard geckos as a food source. Even **pets** such as cats and dogs can pose a threat to leopard geckos when introduced into their natural environment

Are leopard geckos suitable pets for children?

Leopard geckos can be fascinating pets, but their suitability for children depends on a variety of factors. Although some children may be passionate about these reptiles and capable of caring for them responsibly, it is important to consider several aspects before introducing a leopard gecko into a home environment with children. First of all, it is crucial to recognize that leopard geckos are delicate and fragile animals, requiring gentle and careful handling. Young children may have difficulty understanding this necessity and risk unintentionally stressing the animal. Additionally, leopard geckos are generally not animals that enjoy constant handling, which may not meet the expectations of children looking for interactive pets. Specific care, including maintaining an appropriate environment in terms of temperature, humidity and diet, requires special attention and adult supervision. Finally, adopting a leopard gecko is a long-term commitment, as these animals can live for several years in captivity. Children must be prepared to take on this responsibility over the long term, which may require ongoing help and support from parents or guardians.

In conclusion, although leopard geckos can be rewarding pets, their suitability for children depends on many factors and requires careful consideration as well as constant adult supervision to ensure the well-being of both the animal and the family. child.

Are leopard geckos noisy animals?

leopard geckos are generally not noisy animals. Unlike some other reptiles or amphibians that can produce audible sounds, such as frogs, leopard geckos are rather quiet. They do not produce audible vocalizations and are not known to make regular or loud sounds. In general, leopard geckos are relatively calm and discreet animals, making them suitable pets for those who prefer a quiet ambiance in their home environment.

geckos have teeth?

Yes, leopard geckos have teeth, although they are small and often difficult to see. Their teeth are typically conical and arranged along the jaws, helping geckos grasp and manipulate their food. These teeth are used to shred prey, such as insects, before being swallowed. Although leopard geckos do not have teeth as large or as visible as some other animals, their teeth are perfectly adapted to their diet and lifestyle.

Can leopard geckos climb glass surfaces?
leopard geckos are able to climb glass surfaces using their adhesive feet. These legs have millions of tiny hairs called setae , which create adhesive forces through molecular interactions, allowing them to cling to smooth surfaces, including glass. This grip ability allows them to climb vertically on surfaces such as glass terrarium walls. This is one of the fascinating characteristics of leopard geckos that makes them suitable for life in varied environments, including captivity in terrariums.

Can leopard geckos be trained?
Leopard geckos cannot be trained in the same way as dogs or more traditional pets. They do not have the cognitive ability to understand specific commands or behaviors in the same way that mammals do. However, you can establish some familiarity with your leopard gecko by regularly interacting with it in a gentle and calm manner.

Although leopard geckos cannot learn tricks like dogs, they can become accustomed to human presence and can even be trained to recognize signals associated with feeding. For example, by using a consistent diet and regular feeding methods, your gecko can learn to recognize when it's time to eat and come to you when fed.

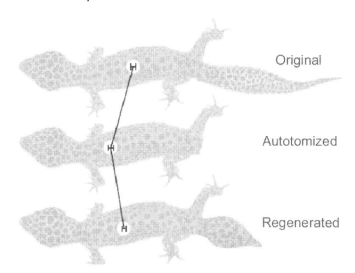

Original

Autotomized

Regenerated

Can leopard geckos lose their tails?

Yes, leopard geckos are capable of losing their tails in a process called autotomy. Autotomy is a defense strategy where the animal voluntarily sacrifices its tail to escape a predator or a dangerous situation. When the tail is detached, it continues to move jerkily, distracting the predator while the gecko escapes.

After losing their tail, leopard geckos can regenerate a new one, although the new tail is usually not as long or as aesthetically pleasing as the original. Additionally, tail regeneration can take several weeks to months, during which the gecko may be more vulnerable to predators due to the loss of this useful appendage.

What is the average price of a leopard gecko?

The average price of a leopard gecko can vary depending on several factors, including age, sex, morphology, genetics, provenance, and rarity of coloring or pattern. In general, the price of a leopard gecko can vary from 20 to 200 euros for a regular individual, but some rarer or high-end specimens can cost more, reaching several hundred euros or even more in some cases.

Can leopard geckos be kept in a terrarium with live plants?

Yes, leopard geckos can be kept in a terrarium with live plants. In fact, live plants can even benefit their well-being by providing a more natural and stimulating environment.

What are the differences between leopard geckos and leopard geckos?

Crested geckos (Correlophus ciliatus) and leopard geckos (Eublepharis macularius) are two species of geckos popular as pets, but they have several important differences:

Characteristic	Crested Geckos	Leopard Geckos
Geographic origin	New Caledonia	Pakistan, Iran, India
Natural habitat	Tropical rainforests, coastal areas	Semi-arid, desert areas
Midsized	20-25cm	Up to 20 cm (body only)
Adhesion to surfaces	Yes (adhesive tabs)	No

Characteristic	Crested Geckos	Leopard Geckos
Diet	Insectivore, frugivore, nectarivore	Insects, worms, small rodents
Habitat requirements	Higher humidity conditions, vertical terrarium	Warmer temperatures, drier substrates

Are leopard geckos prone to parasites?

Yes, leopard geckos can be prone to various parasites, both internal and external, which can affect their health if left untreated. Internal parasites, such as intestinal worms, can cause digestive problems and metabolic disturbances, while external parasites, such as mites and ticks, can cause skin irritations and infections. It is important to monitor leopard geckos regularly for signs of parasite infestation, such as changes in their appearance or behavior, and to consult a reptile veterinarian if necessary. Proper treatment, including antiparasitic medications, may be necessary to eliminate parasites and restore the gecko's health.

Are leopard geckos aggressive?

In general, leopard geckos are not considered aggressive animals towards humans. They are rather shy and reserved animals who tend to avoid direct interactions with humans. However, their behavior can vary between individuals, and some leopard geckos may exhibit defensive behaviors, particularly if they feel threatened or stressed.

When feeling in danger, leopard geckos may exhibit defensive behaviors such as licking their tail, opening their mouth, or even nipping. However, these behaviors are usually used as a deterrent rather than actual aggression.

Do leopard geckos like water?

Leopard geckos are generally not aquatic animals and they do not need to swim or spend time in water like some other reptile species do. However, they require a certain level of humidity to maintain their health and well-being, and they can appreciate moist areas in their environment.

Leopard geckos typically get the humidity they need by licking water off leaves, terrarium walls, or even off their own bodies. They can also be misted regularly to maintain adequate humidity in their habitat. Some leopard geckos may enjoy a shallow bath in a dish of water to rehydrate, but this does not have to be a daily activity.

Can leopard geckos change color ?

Yes, leopard geckos can change color slightly depending on different factors such as temperature, humidity, lighting and their emotional state. Although their ability to change color is not as pronounced as that of some other reptiles, such as chameleons, leopard geckos can exhibit color variations in response to their environment.

For example, a leopard gecko may become lighter or darker depending on the temperature of its environment, as this can affect its activity level and blood circulation. Additionally, a leopard gecko may darken or lighten when stressed or excited, which may be a response to external stimuli. Note that these color changes in leopard geckos are generally subtle and are not as dramatic as in some other animals.

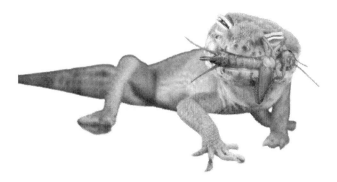

Made in the USA
Las Vegas, NV
14 November 2024

11803631R10015